EXPLORING THE STATES

Mississippi

THE MAGNOLIA STATE

by Blake Hoena

BELLWETHER MEDIA • MINNEAPOLIS, MN

Note to Librarians, Teachers, and Parents:

Blastoff! Readers are carefully developed by literacy experts and combine standards-based content with developmentally appropriate text.

Level 1 provides the most support through repetition of high-frequency words, light text, predictable sentence patterns, and strong visual support.

Level 2 offers early readers a bit more challenge through varied simple sentences, increased text load, and less repetition of high-frequency words.

Level 3 advances early-fluent readers toward fluency through increased text and concept load, less reliance on visuals, longer sentences, and more literary language.

Level 4 builds reading stamina by providing more text per page, increased use of punctuation, greater variation in sentence patterns, and increasingly challenging vocabulary.

Level 5 encourages children to move from "learning to read" to "reading to learn" by providing even more text, varied writing styles, and less familiar topics.

Whichever book is right for your reader, Blastoff! Readers are the perfect books to build confidence and encourage a love of reading that will last a lifetime!

This edition first published in 2014 by Bellwether Media, Inc.

No part of this publication may be reproduced in whole or in part without written permission of the publisher. For information regarding permission, write to Bellwether Media, Inc., Attention: Permissions Department, 5357 Penn Avenue South, Minneapolis, MN 55419.

Library of Congress Cataloging-in-Publication Data

Hoena, B. A.
    Mississippi / by Blake Hoena.
       p. cm. – (Blastoff! readers. Exploring the states)
    Includes bibliographical references and index.
    Summary: "Developed by literacy experts for students in grades three through seven, this book introduces young readers to the geography and culture of Mississippi"–Provided by publisher.
    ISBN 978-1-62617-023-0 (hardcover : alk. paper)
    1. Mississippi–Juvenile literature. I. Title.
    F341.3.H64 2014
    976.2–dc23
                                                                    2013006734

Printed in the United States of America, North Mankato, MN.

Table of Contents

Where Is Mississippi?

Mississippi is located in the southeastern United States. The Mississippi River forms its jagged western border with Louisiana and Arkansas. Tennessee lies to the north, and Alabama is to the east.

Mississippi's southern edge touches the **Gulf** of Mexico. Along the Gulf Coast is the Mississippi **Sound**. **Barrier islands** separate this sound from the Gulf. Jackson, the capital and largest city, stands near the state's center.

Texas

Did you know?

The Mississippi River nearly cuts the United States in half. It flows 2,340 miles (3,766 kilometers) from Minnesota all the way to the Gulf of Mexico.

Tennessee

Southaven

Arkansas

Alabama

Mississippi River

Mississippi

★ Jackson

Louisiana

Hattiesburg

Biloxi

Gulfport

Mississippi Sound

Gulf of Mexico

History

Europeans first explored what is now Mississippi in the 1500s. In the late 1700s, the United States gained control of the area. Mississippi became a state in 1817. It fought for the **Confederacy** during the **Civil War**. The state also played an important role in the **civil rights movement**.

civil rights movement

Mississippi Timeline!

1540: Hernando de Soto is probably the first European to explore the region.

1699: The first permanent settlement is built near Biloxi.

1798: Mississippi Territory is formed.

1817: Mississippi becomes the twentieth state.

1861: Mississippi leaves the Union and joins the Confederate States of America.

1863: The Battle of Vicksburg is fought. The Union gains control of the Mississippi River.

1927: Barriers along the Mississippi River break. This causes the Great Flood of 1927.

1962: James Meredith becomes the first African American to enroll at the University of Mississippi.

1969: The U.S. Supreme Court orders Mississippi schools to desegregate, or end the separation of black and white students.

2005: Hurricane Katrina strikes the Gulf Coast, killing more than 200 Mississippians.

Battle of Vicksburg

Hernando de Soto

Hurricane Katrina damage

Mississippi River

Mississippi can be divided into two main regions. A **floodplain** runs along the Mississippi River. For thousands of years, the river has flooded. It has dumped rich soil onto this narrow stretch of flat land. The area is now home to **fertile** farmlands and vast swamps.

Did you know?
Mississippi is a fairly flat state. Its highest point, Woodall Mountain, is only 806 feet (246 meters) above sea level.

Plains form the eastern part of the state. Rolling hills spread lazily across the land. Forests cover much of this area, while beaches line the southern tip. A string of islands lies off Mississippi's coast. Rain falls often in the state. This makes the weather hot and muggy.

Wetlands

Bogs, swamps, and **marshes** cover more than one-tenth of Mississippi. When rivers flood, water spreads across a floodplain. Over time, the floodwaters create areas of wet, soggy ground called wetlands. Most of the state's bogs and marshes lie along the Mississippi River and the coast.

Wetlands play an important role in nature. They are home to a wealth of wildlife. Everything from large alligators to rare birds, buzzing bugs, and colorful wildflowers live in Mississippi's swamps. Wetlands act as filters that clean water, making it safer to drink. They also work as sponges that soak up water during flooding.

American alligator

Mississippi's forests and swamps create a colorful landscape. Flowering dogwoods and magnolias fill the forests. Cypress trees shoot up through the waters of bayous. Violets and other wildflowers brighten the wetlands.

Did you know?
Mississippi's state reptile is the American alligator. This large predator lurks in the state's swamps and marshes.

Mississippi sandhill crane

red-cockaded woodpecker

leatherback sea turtle

The state is also home to an amazing variety of animals, including many that are **endangered**. Leatherback sea turtles lay their eggs along the Gulf Coast. Mississippi sandhill cranes wade in the wetlands. Red-cockaded woodpeckers nest in tall pine trees. White-tailed deer, opossums, and foxes are all common sights in Mississippi.

Landmarks

Early **native** peoples created a few of Mississippi's landmarks. Emerald Mound is the second largest **burial mound** in the United States. It covers an area the size of nearly seven football fields and stands 35 feet (11 meters) tall. The Natchez Trace Parkway runs diagonally across the state. This historic road follows an 8,000-year-old path that Native Americans once used.

Many Civil War battles took place in Mississippi. One of the most important was fought at Vicksburg in 1863. Nearly 20,000 troops were either killed or wounded. The site of the battle is now a national military park.

Vicksburg

fun fact

In a forest near Flora, ancient trees have turned to stone. They make up the only petrified forest east of the Mississippi River.

Natchez Trace Parkway

Biloxi

Mississippi's first settlement was Fort Maurepas, near present-day Biloxi. Since then, Biloxi has grown into one of the state's larger cities. Lying along the Gulf of Mexico, it provides a relaxing vacation spot for beachgoers and fishers. Visitors are also attracted to the city's many resorts that feature golf courses, fine dining, and **casinos**.

Biloxi
Lighthouse

Biloxi was once Mississippi's third largest city. Then
Hurricane Katrina hit the Gulf Coast in 2005. The storm
damaged hundreds of the homes and businesses. But the
Biloxi Lighthouse, built in 1848, weathered the storm. The
lighthouse has become a sign of hope and survival for
Mississippi's coastal residents.

Many Mississippians work the rich farmland along the floodplain. Broilers are the most common livestock. These are chickens that are raised for their meat. Farmers also raise cattle, sheep, and hogs. Cotton and soybeans are two of Mississippi's main crops. The state's **aqua farms** harvest much of the catfish eaten in the United States.

Factories in Mississippi produce transportation equipment. Food processing plants and furniture companies also employ many people. Oil and natural gas are the state's most important mined products. Most Mississippians have **service jobs**. They work in the state's banks, hotels, and casinos. Many also work for the government.

Where People Work in Mississippi

manufacturing
11%

farming and
natural resources
5%

government
18%

services
66%

Playing

With all the state's waterways, fishing is a favorite pastime in Mississippi. Along the coast, fishers reel in redfish, speckled trout, and snappers. Inland, they fish for black bass, perch, and catfish. Boating and water sports are also popular. Nature lovers trek through wetlands and forests to spot unusual animals and plants.

Did you know?
The first football player to appear on a Wheaties box was Walter Payton in 1986. The Chicago Bears running back was born in Mississippi.

Mississippians do not have a professional sports team to root for. But they are loyal fans of their college teams. The Ole Miss Rebels are based out of Oxford. They have claimed three national football championships. The Mississippi State Bulldogs draw thousands of cheering fans to Starkville.

Mississippi Mud Pie

Ingredients:

1 9-inch baked pie crust

1 stick butter

1 3/4 cups sugar

4 tablespoons cocoa

1/4 cup all purpose flour

4 eggs, beaten

1 teaspoon vanilla extract

3 cups vanilla ice cream, softened

3 tablespoons fudge sauce

Directions:

1. Preheat oven to 350°F.

2. In a bowl, stir together butter, sugar, and cocoa until well combined. Add flour, eggs, and vanilla. Mix until smooth.

3. Pour mixture into crust and bake for 30 to 40 minutes. Remove pie from oven and cool completely.

4. Gently mound ice cream over pie. Freeze until ice cream sets.

5. Drizzle with fudge sauce before serving.

fried catfish

Did you know?

Catfish are also called mudcats because they swim in muddy riverbeds and lake bottoms. They have cat-like "whiskers" called barbels.

seafood boil

In Mississippi, nothing brings a family together like a barbecue. People slow-cook pork ribs in the hot smoke of a fire. They heap their plates with collard greens and mashed potatoes smothered in gravy. Dinner is often washed down with sweet iced tea. For dessert, pecan pie and Mississippi Mud Pie are Southern favorites.

Turnips, **okra**, and sweet potatoes from Mississippi farms are commonly seen at the dinner table. People also gather for seafood boils. These cookouts feature large pots filled with **crawdads** or shrimp along with corn and potatoes. Fried catfish is another state favorite.

Festivals

Mississippi holds several festivals to celebrate the state's history. At the Choctaw Indian Fair, visitors view Native American art and listen to **traditional** music. They can also cheer for their favorite team at stickball games. Every year, a **reenactment** is held at the site of the Battle of Vicksburg. People in costumes act out and tell stories about this famous Civil War battle.

Belzoni is considered the catfish capital of the world. This city holds an annual World Catfish Festival. The event includes a catfish-eating contest, music, and a Miss Catfish pageant.

fun fact

The modern-day sport of lacrosse is based on the traditional game of stickball. In both, players carry sticks with small nets on one end. They use the sticks to pass and shoot a ball.

stickball

Battle of Vicksburg reenactment

The Blues

Music is as much a part of Mississippi as catfish and the Civil War. During the 1800s, African-American **slaves** would sing along with the rhythms of their work. Over time, these work chants blended with folk songs and **spirituals**. A unique style of music called the blues was born.

Muddy Waters

B.B. King

Blues artists sing about sadness and suffering over a twanging guitar. The piano and harmonica are other common blues instruments. B.B. King, Bo Diddley, and Muddy Waters are some of the famous bluesmen from Mississippi. These great musicians helped create Mississippi's rich culture.

Mississippi's Flag

The top left of Mississippi's flag features the "union square." This is similar to the Confederate Flag that was used in battle during the Civil War. The 13 stars on this part of the flag are said to represent the 13 Confederate States. The flag's blue, white, and red stripes mimic the colors of the U.S. flag.

State Flower
magnolia blossom

State Nicknames:	The Magnolia State
	The Mudcat State
State Motto:	*Virtute et Armis*; "By Valor and Arms"
Year of Statehood:	1817
Capital City:	Jackson
Other Major Cities:	Gulfport, Southaven, Hattiesburg
Population:	2,967,297 (2010)
Area:	47,692 square miles (123,522 square kilometers); Mississippi is the 32nd largest state.
Major Industries:	farming, manufacturing, mining, services
Natural Resources:	farmland, oil, natural gas
State Government:	122 representatives; 52 senators
Federal Government:	4 representatives; 2 senators
Electoral Votes:	6

State Bird
northern mockingbird

State Animal
red fox

Glossary

aqua farms—farms that raise seafood such as catfish

barrier islands—narrow, sandy islands that run next to a mainland coast

bogs—areas of wet, spongy ground

burial mound—a heap of earth constructed over tombs by ancient people

casinos—buildings where people bet money on games of chance

civil rights movement—the effort to gain equal rights for African Americans; the civil rights movement took place in the United States in the 1950s and 1960s.

Civil War—a war between the Northern (Union) and Southern (Confederate) states that lasted from 1861 to 1865

Confederacy—the group of southern states that formed a new country in the early 1860s; they fought against the northern states during the Civil War.

crawdads—crayfish; crayfish are shellfish that look like lobsters.

endangered—at risk of becoming extinct

fertile—able to support growth

floodplain—a low area near a river or stream that often floods

gulf—part of an ocean or sea that extends into land

marshes—wetlands with grasses and plants

native—originally from a specific place

okra—a green vegetable with a slippery texture

plains—large areas of flat land

reenactment—the performance of a historic event

service jobs—jobs that perform tasks for people or businesses

slaves—people who are considered property; African Americans were bought and sold as slaves in the Southern United States until the late 1800s.

sound—a long, wide extension of the ocean into land

spirituals—religious folk songs

traditional—relating to a custom, idea, or belief handed down from one generation to the next

To Learn More

AT THE LIBRARY

Casil, Amy Sterling. *Mississippi: Past and Present.* New York, N.Y.: Rosen Central, 2011.

Foran, Jill. *Mississippi: The Magnolia State.* New York, N.Y.: Weigl, 2012.

O'Neal, Claire. *The Mississippi River.* Hockessin, Del.: Mitchell Lane Publishers, 2013.

ON THE WEB

Learning more about Mississippi is as easy as 1, 2, 3.

1. Go to www.factsurfer.com.

2. Enter "Mississippi" into the search box.

3. Click the "Surf" button and you will see a list of related Web sites.

With factsurfer.com, finding more information is just a click away.

Index

The images in this book are reproduced through the courtesy of: JayL, front cover (bottom);
Everett Collection Historical/ Alamy, p. 6; Archive Images/ Alamy, p. 7 (left); Illustrated History/
Alamy, p. 7 (middle); Robert A. Mansker, p. 7 (right); Sue120502, pp. 8-9; Radius Images/ Glow
Images, pp. 10-11; Fritz Pölking/ Mauritius/ SuperStock, pp. 12-13; Dennis Donohue, p. 13 (top);
Feathercollector, p. 13 (middle); Frans Lemmens/ SuperStock, p. 13 (bottom); Age Fotostock/
SuperStock, pp. 14-15, 14 (top); Csarsene/ Wikipedia, p. 14 (bottom); DenisTangneyJr, pp. 16-17,
17 (top); David R. Frazier/ DanitaDelimont.com "Danita Delimont Photography/ Newscom, p. 17
(bottom); Zuma Press, Inc./ Alamy, p. 18; Dennis MacDonald/ Age Fotostock/ SuperStock, p. 19;
Nomad/ SuperStock, p. 20; Spruce Derden/ Zumapress/ Newscom, pp. 20-21; Simon Reddy/
Alamy, p. 22; Adlifemarketing, p. 23 (top); Lori Monahan Borden, p. 23 (bottom); Copyright
Bettmann/ Corbis/ AP Images/ Associated Press, p. 24; James P. Blair/ Contributor/ Getty Images,
pp. 24-25; Hemis/ Alamy, pp. 26-27; Everett Collection Historical/ Alamy, p. 27 (top); Akg/ Jazz
Archiv Hamburg/ Newscom, p. 27 (bottom); Carsten Reisinger, p. 28 (top); Melinda Fawver, p. 28
(bottom); Michael J Thompson, p. 29 (left); Eric Isselee, p. 29 (right).